D1483520

SQUID

A Buddy Book by
Deborah Coldiron

ABDO
Publishing Company

UNDERWATER WORLD

VISIT US AT
www.abdopublishing.com

Published by ABDO Publishing Company, 8000 West 78th Street, Edina, Minnesota 55435.

Printed in the United States.

Coordinating Series Editor: Sarah Tieck
Contributing Editor: Michael P. Goecke
Graphic Design: Deborah Coldiron
Cover Photograph: Minden Pictures: Chris Newbert
Interior Photographs/Illustrations: Animals Animals - Earth Scenes: Bob Cranston (pages 15, 23); Art Explosion (page 21); Clipart.com (pages 11, 29); Brandon Cole Marine Photography (pages 7, 19); Corbis (page 20); Getty Images/AFP: STF/Staff (page 30); ImageMix (page 21); Minden Pictures: Norbert Wu (pages 13, 28); Photos.com (pages 5, 7, 9, 20, 21, 25, 27)

Library of Congress Cataloging-in-Publication Data

Coldiron, Deborah.
   Squid / Deborah Coldiron.
      p. cm. — (Underwater World)
   Includes index.
   ISBN 978-1-59928-816-1
   1. Squids—Juvenile literature. I. Title.

QL430.2.C49 2007
594'.58—dc22

                                    2007014855

Table Of Contents

The World Of Squid 4

Get A Little Closer 10

Which Is Bigger? 16

A Growing Squid 18

Family Matters 20

Powerful Predators 22

Danger Zone 24

Fascinating Facts 28

Learn And Explore 30

Important Words 31

Web Sites 31

Index 32

The World Of Squid

Every living creature needs water. Some animals not only need water, they live in it, too.

Scientists have found more than 250,000 kinds of plants and animals living underwater. And, they believe there could be one million more! The squid is one animal that lives in this underwater world.

Seventy percent of Earth's surface is covered in water.

Squid are **torpedo**-shaped creatures with soft bodies and many arms. There are more than 400 kinds of squid on Earth.

Squid come in many sizes. The smallest squid is less than one inch (3 cm) long. The largest may grow up to 60 feet (18 m) long!

There is a wide variety of colors and patterns among the world's squid populations.

Squid cannot live in freshwater. They make their homes throughout the world's oceans. They're found everywhere from warm, shallow areas to the cold depths of the sea.

Squid spend most of their time swimming. Sometimes they hunt for prey. Other times, they swim fast or hide to avoid predators. Their bodies are designed to move quickly and easily.

Many species of squid travel together in large groups called shoals.

There may be thousands of squid in a single shoal.

Get A Little Closer

Squid are **invertebrates**. The main part of a squid's body is bullet shaped. It is called a mantle.

To move, a squid takes water into its mantle. Then, it forces the water out through a tube called a siphon. The siphon can be aimed in many directions. This helps the squid control which way it moves.

FAST FACTS Squid are the world's fastest moving invertebrates.

The Body of a Squid

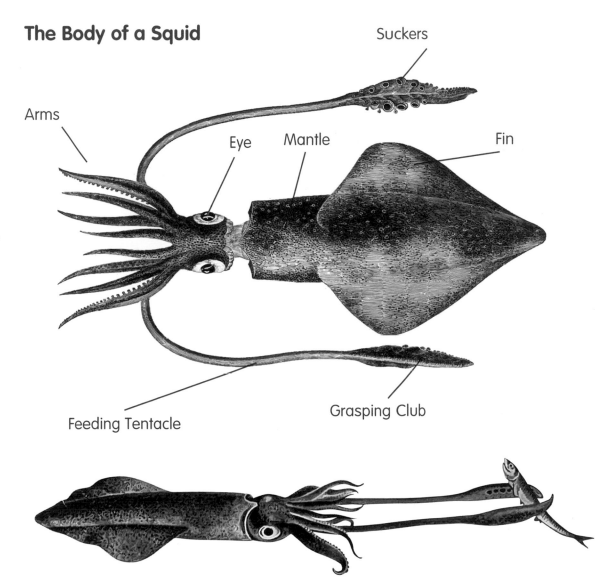

Suckers

Arms

Eye

Mantle

Fin

Feeding Tentacle

Grasping Club

Feeding tentacles and grasping clubs in action

⠶⠐

Most squid have ten arms that are lined with many suckers. Two of their arms are often much longer than the others. These special arms are called feeding **tentacles**. Squid use them to grab their food.

A squid's mouth is surrounded by its many arms. The mouth has a pair of beaklike jaws. The squid uses its jaws to bite off chunks of flesh from its prey.

Some squid's suckers are lined with sawlike teeth.

Inside the squid's mouth, there is a rough tongue called a radula. This helps cut the squid's food and move it to the stomach.

Squid eyes are very similar to human eyes. And, squid have excellent eyesight.

Squid also have well-developed brains. Scientists consider them to be among the world's smartest animals.

FAST FACTS

The giant squid may have the largest eyes in the world. They are about the size of a basketball!

Some squid eyes have a cornea over the lens, like human eyes. Squid without corneas have protective eyelids.

Which Is Bigger?

Scientists have long wanted to see a live giant squid. In 2004, two Japanese scientists dangled a camera and bait more than a half-mile (1 km) deep. A giant squid grabbed the bait.

In 2007, some fishermen working near Antarctica caught a colossal squid. It was even bigger than the giant squid!

The colossal squid is the true squid giant of the sea. It looks bulky. It has shorter arms. But, its mantle is longer and wider than that of the giant squid. The giant squid is long and slender.

Giant Squid Vs. Colossal Squid

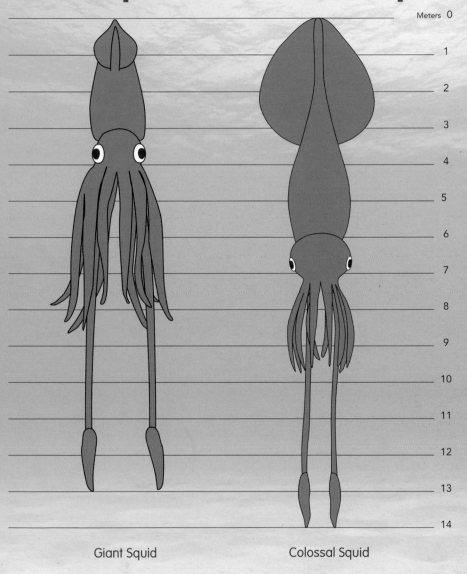

	Meters 0
	1
	2
	3
	4
	5
	6
	7
	8
	9
	10
	11
	12
	13
	14

Giant Squid   Colossal Squid

A Growing Squid

Squid mothers lay their egg cases on the ocean floor in clusters. These are called mops. Most squid mothers do not care for their eggs.

Each finger-shaped egg case holds 150 to 300 eggs. Squid hatch as tiny larvae. Then, they grow quickly to full size.

Squid have short life spans. Some squid live less than a year. While others live up to a few years.

FAST FACTS

Scientists have discovered one type of squid that takes care of her eggs. This deep-sea dweller carries her eggs in an egg sac as big as her body! She can't eat during the entire nine months of carrying her eggs!

This is a cluster of squid eggs. Many female squid become weak after laying their eggs. In fact, most of them die shortly after.

Family Matters

Squid belong to a group of animals called cephalopods. Cephalopods have soft bodies and many arms. They are some of the most intelligent creatures in the sea.

There are around 800 known **species** of cephalopods. This group includes octopuses, nautiluses, and cuttlefish.

Octopuses have eight arms and no feeding tentacles.

Cuttlefish are known for quickly changing color. Unlike other cephalopods, they have a hard plate inside their bodies. This is a cuttlebone.

Unlike other cephalopods, nautiluses have a hard shell. Some have as many as 90 arms! Their arms do not have suckers.

The blue ring octopus is one of the most poisonous animals in the ocean. Its numbing venom is more powerful than any land animal's venom.

Octopuses are famous for their ability to use camouflage to hide. They can change their skin color and texture to stay out of sight from predators.

The flamboyant cuttlefish is small but deadly. It is only about two inches (5 cm) long, but its flesh is toxic.

Powerful Predators

Squid are very capable predators. They eat many kinds of fish, shellfish, and **plankton**. Scientists believe that some squid, such as the giant squid, may even eat other squid!

Squid attack their prey in quick jolts. Their feeding **tentacles** shoot out in front of them to capture prey. Some squid even have poison **glands** they use to stun other animals.

Humboldt squid eat prey such as fish. They use their beaklike jaws to tear food into small pieces that can be easily swallowed.

Danger Zone

Many animals depend on squid as their major food source. Whales, sharks, seals, and many kinds of fish hunt squid. There are even birds and crabs that eat squid. Humans eat squid, too.

Birds such as albatross (*left*), petrels (*right*), and pelicans (*bottom*) eat squid.

To help protect them from predators, squid perform special tricks. Their bodies help them hide and escape.

Squid have ink sacs inside their bodies. When they feel **threatened**, they can shoot out ink. The ink turns clear water cloudy and helps the squid escape.

Some people enjoy dried squid as a chewy snack. Others include it in stir-frys. Squid ink is also used in cooking. It adds both flavor and color to foods such as rice and pasta.

Squid can also change their skin color. Some squid even give off light. These abilities help them hide. They also cause confusion, which helps squid escape.

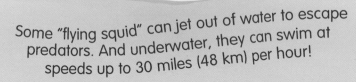

Some "flying squid" can jet out of water to escape predators. And underwater, they can swim at speeds up to 30 miles (48 km) per hour!

Fascinating Facts

🦑 Squid have three hearts! Two hearts supply the gills with blood. The third pumps blood through the squid's body.

🦑 Humboldt squid are also known as red devils. This name comes from the many stories of squid attacking fishers near the coast of Mexico.

Humboldt squid are also called jumbo flying squid. These squid can shoot out of the water while fleeing from enemies.

🦑 Many years ago, fishermen feared a sea monster they called the Kraken. They said it could wrap its long arms around a ship and drag it into the sea. Today, people think the legendary Kraken was actually a very large squid!

Throughout the years, several stories, poems, and works of art have been inspired by the legend of the Kraken.

Learn And Explore

Many people have searched for live giant squid. But, marine biologist Steve O'Shea decided to grow one.

O'Shea collected giant squid larvae. Today, he is trying to grow them in his New Zealand lab.

This experiment is a first. Hopefully, it will help people learn about giant squid!

Steve O'Shea examining the body of a giant squid.

IMPORTANT WORDS

gland   a part of the body that produces a fluid.

invertebrate   an animal without a backbone.

plankton   tiny animals and plants that float in the sea.

species   living things that are very much alike.

tentacle   a long, slender body part that grows around the mouth or the head of some animals.

threat   something that could be harmful.

torpedo   a long, rounded missile that is fired underwater.

WEB SITES

To learn more about squid, visit ABDO Publishing Company on the World Wide Web. Web sites about squid are featured on our Book Links page. These links are routinely monitored and updated to provide the most current information available.

www.abdopublishing.com

INDEX

Antarctica **16**

arms **6, 11, 12, 16, 20, 29**

blood **28**

brain **14**

cephalopod **20, 21**

color **7, 27**

colossal squid **12, 16, 17**

eggs **18, 19**

eyes **11, 14, 15**

fin **11**

fishers **16, 29**

flamboyant cuttlefish **21**

food **12, 14, 22, 23**

giant squid **14, 16, 17, 22, 30**

gills **28**

grasping clubs **11**

heart **28**

hooks **12**

Humboldt squid **23, 28**

ink sac **26**

invertebrates **10**

Kraken **29**

life cycle **18, 19**

mantle **10, 11, 16**

Mexico **28**

mouth **12, 14**

New Zealand **30**

O'Shea, Steve **30**

poison glands **22**

radula **14**

shoal **8, 9**

siphon **10**

skin **27**

stomach **14**

suckers **11, 12, 13**

teeth **13**

tentacles **11, 12, 22**